BEN & KATIE

BY DOUG BAKER and HERNANDEZ

© 1989 Express Newspapers plc.
Ludgate House, 245 Blackfriars Road,
London SE1 9UX

AN EXPRESS
BOOKS PUBLICATION

Printed by Grosvenor Press (Portsmouth), England and co-ordinated
by Roeder Print Services Limited

£1.95

BEN & KATIE

From the DAILY STAR

THIS COMPANY I WORK FOR ARE REAL MEAN. THEY PAY ME NEXT TO NOTHING
THEN WHY DO YOU CARRY ON WINDOW CLEANING?
JOB SATISFACTION, LOVE
164
© EXPRESS NEWSPAPERS p.l.c. 1988
MIKE'S BEEN MARRIED FIVE TIMES, YOU KNOW, AND HAS SEVEN CHILDREN FROM THE MARRIAGES
ARE YOU GOING TO MARRY HIM?
I'D LOVE TO BUT HE SAYS HE'S NOT READY TO SETTLE DOWN YET
© EXPRESS NEWSPAPERS p.l.c. 1988
81

IS THAT NEW JACKIE ROBBINS NOVEL AS STEAMY AND EROTIC AS HER OTHERS?
STEAMY? LISTEN, DON'T GET THE EXPURGATED VERSION
WHY NOT?
THERE'S ONLY THE PUNCTUATION LEFT
© EXPRESS NEWSPAPERS p.l.c. 1988
59

DON'T FORGET—WE'RE LOOKING FOR SOMEWHERE THAT'S UNSPOILT
THIS IS JUST THE PLACE FOR YOU. YOU'LL LOVE IT
IS IT COMPLETELY UNSPOILT?
MADAM, IT'S SO UNSPOILT THEY HAVEN'T STARTED BUILDING YOUR HOTEL YET
© EXPRESS NEWSPAPERS p.l.c. 1988
60

WE'RE GOING TO LONDON TO SEE AN EXHIBITION ON RAIL TECHNOLOGY. THE SPEEDS TRAINS CAN ACHIEVE NOWADAYS IS BREATHTAKING

WILL YOU TRAVEL TO LONDON BY TRAIN?

NO, COACH—IT'S QUICKER

I'VE BEEN FIGHTING MY TIREDNESS BY TAKING IRON TABLETS, GINSENG, VITAMIN C, TONICS ....

...AMICA, KALI PHOS, SEPIA, ARSENICUM ALBUM ....
AND DO YOU FEEL BETTER?

NO, THE ENDLESS TRIPS TO THE HEALTH FOOD SHOP ARE MAKING ME MORE TIRED

232

THAT UNGRATEFUL BANK MANAGER! HE REFUSED ME AN OVERDRAFT!

© EXPRESS NEWSPAPERS p.l.c. 1988
AND AFTER ALL THE MONEY I'VE WITHDRAWN FROM THAT BANK! SO I TOLD HIM IF HE DIDN'T GIVE ME AN OVERDRAFT ...

235
... I'D TAKE MY ACCOUNT TO A BANK THAT WOULD!

© EXPRESS NEWSPAPERS p.l.c. 1988
MY NEW SWIMSUIT, DARLING. IT WAS ONLY £45

£45 FOR THAT! AS SWIMSUIT MATERIAL DECREASES, THE PRICE INCREASES

I WONDER HOW MUCH THEY'LL CHARGE WHEN THEY DON'T USE ANY MATERIAL AT ALL
169

I'VE BOUGHT A TELEPHONE ANSWERING SERVICE — IDEAL FOR CALLERS WHILE WE'RE OUT

THERE ARE FOUR MORE OVER THERE. WHAT ARE THEY FOR?

IN CASE YOUR MOTHER PHONES
© EXPRESS NEWSPAPERS p.l.c. 1988
187

WHEN I REACHED THIRTY, I CRIED MY EYES OUT BECAUSE I JUST DIDN'T WANT TO BE THIRTY
© EXPRESS NEWSPAPERS p.l.c. 1988

AND HERE YOU ARE ON YOUR FORTIETH BIRTHDAY CRYING AGAIN. WHY?

BECAUSE I DO WANT TO BE THIRTY
188

ROGER GOT A LITTLE TOO AMOROUS LAST NIGHT

I TOLD HIM I WASN'T GOING TO DO THAT SORT OF THING TILL AFTER I WAS MARRIED
© EXPRESS NEWSPAPERS p.l.c. 1988

SO HE TOLD ME TO LET HIM KNOW WHEN I WAS MARRIED AND HE'D POP ROUND
209

I'M GOING TO BACK THE FAVOURITE EACH WAY
© EXPRESS NEWSPAPERS p.l.c. 1988

I'M GOING TO BACK IT ONLY ONE WAY...

...IT DOESN'T LOOK STRONG ENOUGH TO MAKE THE RETURN JOURNEY
210

I DON'T EXPECT YOU TO BRING ME IN A LOVELY BUNCH OF ROSES THIS EVENING, DARLING
ALL RIGHT, I WON'T
THAT'S NOT A VERY NICE THING TO SAY!
BUT YOU SAID YOU DIDN'T EXPECT—
OF COURSE I'M NOT EXPECTING THEM—I WANT THEM TO BE A SURPRISE
© EXPRESS NEWSPAPERS p.l.c. 1988
54
YOU KNOW MR. WAGSTAFF, THE MAN WITH ELEVEN CHILDREN? THE DOCTOR'S TOLD HIM HE NEEDS MORE EXERCISE 
YOU SURPRISE ME. DID THE DOCTOR TELL HIM HOW TO GO ABOUT IT?
© EXPRESS NEWSPAPERS p.l.c. 1988
YES, HE TOLD HIM TO GET RID OF HIS DOUBLE BED AND GET TWIN BEDS
113

JUST A GLASS OF MILK, PLEASE

CERTAINLY, MADAM. I'LL BRING YOU A PLATE AS WELL
A PLATE?

OR YOU'LL HAVE NOTHING TO LEAVE THE TIP UNDER
107

HAVE YOU ANY IDEA HOW MUCH TIME YOU TWO WASTE WATCHING THIS RUBBISH ON TELEVISION? YOU OUGHT TO KNOW BETTER!

ANYWAY, I'VE GOT TO GO NOW

WHERE'S SHE OFF TO?
BINGO
90

I WENT SHOPPING YESTERDAY. I WAS LOOKING FOR SOMETHING FAR FROM CHEAP, BUT EXCLUSIVE, THAT I COULD GET A LOT OF USE OUT OF

LIKE TO SEE WHAT I GOT?
YES, WE WOULD

HENRY, COME AND MEET BEN AND KATIE
© EXPRESS NEWSPAPERS p.l.c. 1988
75

THE SERVICE HERE IS VERY GOOD
© EXPRESS NEWSPAPERS p.l.c. 1988

PLEASE BE SEATED, MADAM

I CAN RECOMMEND THE GAME PIE AND STRAWBERRIES, MADAM, FOLLOWED BY SHERRY TRIFLE AND ONIONS
66

EXCUSE ME.
THIS NO. 513 ROUTE
—ARE THE BUSES
FREQUENT?
© EXPRESS NEWSPAPERS p.l.c. 1988

ABOUT AS FREQUENT
AS LEAP YEARS

WE'RE IN
LUCK—THERE
SHOULD BE
ONE ALONG
ANY MONTH
NOW

IT'S TRUE. I SHALL HAVE TO GO
OUT AND BUY A COUPLE OF
DRESSES
I HAVEN'T
GOT A
THING TO
WEAR!
WHERE HAVE I
HEARD THAT
BEFORE?
© EXPRESS NEWSPAPERS p.l.c. 1988
79

BUT WHERE
WILL I KEEP THEM
— THE WARDROBE'S
FULL

THAT GERMAN SHIPPING TYCOON — IT'S HIS BIRTHDAY TODAY. WONDER WHAT HIS WIFE WILL GIVE HIM
© EXPRESS NEWSPAPERS p.l.c. 1983

WHAT WOULD YOU GIVE A MAN WHO'S GOT EVERYTHING?

249
MY TELEPHONE NUMBER

I REFUSE TO BECOME A HOUSEHOLD SLAVE, A SKIVVY AT THE BECK AND CALL OF MALE CHAUVINISTS!
© EXPRESS NEWSPAPERS p.l.c. 1988

250
IT'S DEGRADING, HUMILIATING! WHY SHOULD I WAIT ON YOU HAND AND FOOT?

LOOK, ALL I DID WAS ASK YOU TO SHOW ME WHERE YOU KEEP THE WASHING-UP LIQUID

IT WAS CHAOS IN THE SALES YESTERDAY, DARLING, BUT I MANAGED TO GET A LOVELY LITTLE TOP
© EXPRESS NEWSPAPERS p.l.c. 1988

WHAT DID IT COST YOU?

THE NEW COAT I WAS WEARING THAT GOT RIPPED AND RUINED IN THE STAMPEDE
233

I'VE LAID OUT YOUR LIGHT TROUSERS FOR YOU, DARLING
© EXPRESS NEWSPAPERS p.l.c. 1988
242

I DIDN'T KNOW I'D GOT ANY LIGHT TROUSERS

YOU HAVE NOW I'VE EMPTIED THE POCKETS

THAT'S MRS. DAWSON DRIVING PAST. SHE NEVER STOPS TALKING

THE TYPE THAT LIKES TO HAVE THE LAST WORD, IS SHE?
© EXPRESS NEWSPAPERS p.l.c. 1988

NOBODY KNOWS— SHE'S NEVER GOT TO IT YET
157

WHY ALL THIS TIME GETTING READY, THIS SPECIAL PREPARATION— WE'RE ONLY GOING TO THE SUPERMARKET
© EXPRESS NEWSPAPERS p.l.c. 1988
HAVEN'T YOU HEARD, DARLING?

THEY'VE INSTALLED SECURITY TELEVISION CAMERAS
158

A MAN IN THE TORA HOTEL GRABBED ME AND TRIED TO HAVE HIS OWN WAY WITH ME

DID HE SUCCEED?
NO, HE DIDN'T

TRY THE ZICO HOTEL
177

217
ARE YOU GOING FOR A RECORD? YOU'VE BEEN AN HOUR GETTING READY AND YOU'VE ONLY GOT THIS FAR

LET ME KNOW WHEN YOU'RE READY
I'M READY NOW, DARLING

THAT'S WHAT I WANTED TO HEAR — NOW I KNOW YOU'LL BE READY IN ANOTHER TWENTY MINUTES

THE POLICE LEANED ON ME AND FORCED ME TO TELL THEM WHAT I KNEW ABOUT THE BANK ROBBERY

207
HOW DID THEY LEAN ON YOU?
© EXPRESS NEWSPAPERS p.l.c. 1988

THEY THREATENED TO PUT ME IN THE WITNESS BOX AND MAKE ME STATE MY AGE

I WAS ABSOLUTELY FURIOUS WITH MY DRIVING INSTRUCTOR THIS MORNING WHEN HE CRITICISED MY DRIVING
© EXPRESS NEWSPAPERS p.l.c. 1988

WHY DIDN'T YOU GET OUT OF THE CAR AND LEAVE HIM?

248
I CAN'T SWIM

I DIDN'T TAKE TO SIR ROGER AT FIRST, KATIE, BUT I MARRIED HIM WHEN I DISCOVERED HE HAD HIDDEN QUALITIES

52
WHAT HIDDEN QUALITIES?
© EXPRESS NEWSPAPERS p.l.c. 1988

BANK ACCOUNTS IN ZURICH

AN OLD TRAMP CALLED THIS MORNING
© EXPRESS NEWSPAPERS p.l.c. 1988

HE SAID HE HADN'T HAD A DECENT MEAL IN WEEKS, SO I GAVE HIM A FIVER

IN THAT CASE, I'LL EXPECT YOU TO GIVE ME A HANDFUL OF FIVERS
125

ISN'T MY BOYFRIEND LUCKY? HE'LL BE MARRYING THE LOVELIEST GIRL IN THE WORLD
© EXPRESS NEWSPAPERS p.l.c. 1988

HE CERTAINLY IS

244
WHO IS SHE?

IF YOU WERE REINCARNATED, WHAT FORM WOULD YOU LIKE TO RETURN IN?
I'D LIKE TO BE A MINK
92

AN ANIMAL THAT LOOKS LIKE A WEASEL? WHY?
REINCARNATION
© EXPRESS NEWSPAPERS p.l.c. 1988

IT'S THE ONLY WAY I'M EVER LIKELY TO GET A MINK COAT

I SET THE ALARM CLOCK FOR SEVEN, THEN PUT THE SNOOZE ALARM ON FOR TEN MINUTES LATER ...

... AND FOR EXTRA PRECAUTION I GOT THE MILKMAN AND THE POSTMAN TO GIVE US A KNOCK
SO WHY WERE YOU LATE?

WE OVERSLEPT

I SEE OUR LOCAL FOOTBALL TEAM IS BEING SPONSORED BY A BREWERY

YES, THEY'RE PRETTY SHREWD THESE BREWERS
WHAT DO YOU MEAN?

WELL, THE WAY THE LOCAL TEAM'S PLAYING THEY MUST BE DRIVING ALL THE SUPPORTERS TO DRINK

YOU AND YOUR BIG MOUTH, KATIE
MEANING WHAT?

YOU COMPLAINED TO THE LOCAL COUNCIL ABOUT THE NEIGHBOURHOOD BECOMING SHODDY AND LOSING ITS AFFLUENT IMAGE AND SUGGESTED THEY DO SOMETHING ABOUT IT
SO?
© EXPRESS NEWSPAPERS p.l.c. 1988

SO THEY'RE GOING TO— THEY'RE GOING TO PUT THE RATES UP!
208

THERE'S LIZA OVER THERE. I DETEST AND DESPISE HER! SHE MAKES MY BLOOD BOIL, THE ODIOUS ANIMAL!

SHE'S THE MOST OBNOXIOUS PERSON I'VE EVER MET! YOU'RE LUCKY NOT TO KNOW HER— SHE'S VILE!
WHICH ONE IS LIZA?
© EXPRESS NEWSPAPERS p.l.c. 1988

204
THE ONE IN THE DRESS THAT'S IDENTICAL TO MINE!

TELL ME WHAT THE BIRTHDAY SURPRISE IS YOU'VE GOT FOR ME, DARLING

LOOK, IF I TOLD YOU WHAT IT IS, IT WOULDN'T BE A SURPRISE

IT WOULD IF YOU TOLD ME, THEN SURPRISED ME WITH A SECOND PRESENT
135

YOU SHOULD COMPLAIN
I WAS LIVID IN THE POST OFFICE TODAY. I HAD TO QUEUE FOR TWENTY MINUTES FOR A POSTAL ORDER AND THEN FIFTEEN MINUTES AT THE PARCEL COUNTER!

140
COMPLAIN? HAVE YOU SEEN THE LENGTH OF THE COMPLAINTS QUEUE?

HOW CAN WE GET RID OF THIS HIDEOUS VASE AUNT EDITH GAVE US, WITHOUT OFFENDING HER?

WE'LL SAY BURGLARS STOLE IT

BURGLARS STOLE IT? RUBBISH! I WAS BURGLED FOUR TIMES AND THEY NEVER TOUCHED THE HIDEOUS THING!
© EXPRESS NEWSPAPERS p.l.c. 1988
103

HAS YOUR WIFE GOT A FEW OLD CLOTHES SHE CAN SPARE FOR THE JUMBLE SALE, BEN?
I'M AFRAID NOT
© EXPRESS NEWSPAPERS p.l.c. 1988

BUT SURELY SHE'S GOT SOMETHING
NO, SHE HASN'T

BEN, I HAVEN'T GOT A THING TO WEAR

SEE WHAT I MEAN?
98

DID YOU SEE THIS? AT A CAMBRIDGE MATERNITY HOSPITAL, A FIFTH OF THE STAFF ARE PREGNANT OR HAVE HAD BABIES RECENTLY
© EXPRESS NEWSPAPERS p.l.c. 1988

ARE YOU SURE IT'S A MATERNITY HOSPITAL ...

... AND NOT A HOSPITAL FOR CONTAGIOUS ILLNESSES?
67

THANK HEAVENS SHE'S GONE! THAT TONGUE OF HERS NEVER STOPS WAGGING
© EXPRESS NEWSPAPERS p.l.c. 1988

I'VE NEVER KNOWN ANYONE TALK AS MUCH AS SHE DOES

62
IF SHE INTERRUPTED ME ONCE, SHE INTERRUPTED ME FIFTY TIMES!

AS WE'RE SHORT OF MONEY, DID YOU DO AS I SUGGESTED AND NOT SPEND ANYTHING?

OF COURSE, DARLING
CAN YOU PROVE IT?
© EXPRESS NEWSPAPERS p.l.c. 1988

YES—I'LL GET THE BILLS
165

NEVER AGAIN SHALL WE TRAVEL NORTH ON THE A1 ON A FRIDAY EVENING!

WE'VE BEEN STUCK IN THIS TAILBACK FOR HOURS!
© EXPRESS NEWSPAPERS p.l.c. 1988

NOW WE KNOW WHAT THEY MEAN BY 'LIVING IN THE FAST LANE!'
161

THAT NEW DRESS I BOUGHT, NICOLA — BEN WANTS ME TO CHANGE IT BECAUSE IT'S TOO REVEALING

I THINK IT SUITS YOU. WHAT DID IT REVEAL?
© EXPRESS NEWSPAPERS p.l.c. 1988

THE PRICE
50

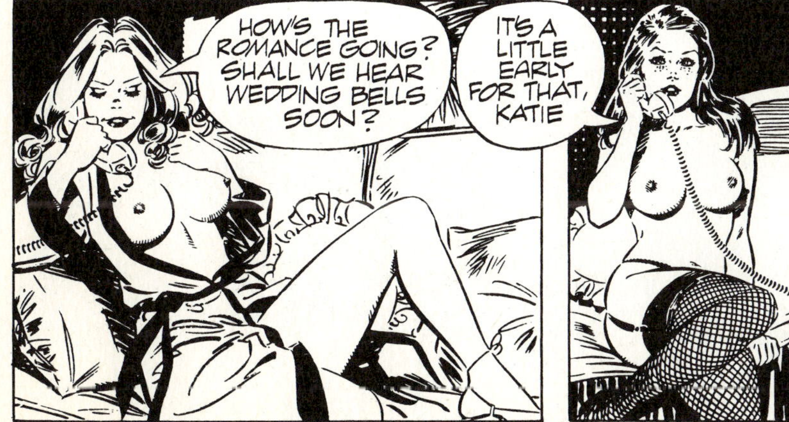

HOW'S THE ROMANCE GOING? SHALL WE HEAR WEDDING BELLS SOON?
IT'S A LITTLE EARLY FOR THAT, KATIE
© EXPRESS NEWSPAPERS p.l.c. 1988
159

I CAN'T LEAD HIM UP THE AISLE YET — I'M STILL LEADING HIM UP THE GARDEN PATH

THIS IS MY NEW BIKINI FOR THE BEACH, DARLING

DO YOU THINK IT WILL MAKE MALE EYES WORK OVERTIME?
© EXPRESS NEWSPAPERS p.l.c. 1988

IT PROBABLY WILL, BUT NEVER MIND — THEIR IMAGINATIONS WILL HAVE A REST
86

HELLO, TRACIE. HOW'S THAT BOYFRIEND OF YOURS — THE ONE WITH EYES LIKE PAUL NEWMAN, LIPS LIKE RICHARD GERE, HAIR LIKE ROBERT REDFORD AND BODY LIKE BURT REYNOLDS?
© EXPRESS NEWSPAPERS p.l.c. 1988

HE NEVER SEES ME NOW
WHAT STOPS HIM FROM SEEING YOU?

THE ROVING INSTINCTS OF WARREN BEATTY
82

WHAT'S HAPPENED TO JOE, MY REGULAR WINDOW CLEANER?
GONE TO GET HIS GLASSES MENDED. I ALWAYS DO YOUR WINDOWS WHEN HE CAN'T MAKE IT
REAL VIOLENCE IS CAUSED BY PEOPLE WHO ARE INFLUENCED BY VIOLENCE ON T.V.

WHAT HAPPENED TO HIS GLASSES?
© EXPRESS NEWSPAPERS p.l.c. 1988
THEY COULD EASILY STAMP IT OUT
HOW?
© EXPRESS NEWSPAPERS p.l.c. 1988

HE PUT THEM ON THE TABLE AND I ACCIDENTALLY TROD ON THEM
CALL IN THE A-TEAM

NICE PARTY, PAUL, BUT NOBODY DRANK MUCH. YOU'VE GOT A LOT OF DRINK LEFT OVER

WHAT'S THE SECRET OF A SUCCESSFUL PARTY ?

ONLY INVITE PEOPLE WHO LIVE MILES AWAY— THEY CAN'T DRINK AND DRIVE

YOU'VE APPEARED AT THAT WINDOW EVERY TIME I'VE TAKEN A BATH FOR THE PAST TWO WEEKS

I HOPE IT'S NOT GOING TO GO ON

OF COURSE NOT, LOVE— ONLY TILL THAT LITTLE REDHEAD AT No. 57 GETS BACK FROM HER HOLIDAY

I CAN'T SLEEP, DARLING

I'VE GOT JUST THE CURE FOR IT, ANGEL

LATER....
THAT PROBLEM I GAVE YOU THE CURE FOR AN HOUR AGO — IT'S CONTAGIOUS!

I DON'T WANT TO QUESTION HER AGE, BUT SURELY THERE SHOULD BE MORE CANDLES ON HER CAKE

DARLING, AT HER AGE...

...THERE SHOULD BE MORE CAKE TO PUT THE CANDLES ON!

EEEK! I JUST SAW A GREY HAIR!
YOU OUGHT TO BE ABLE TO ACCEPT A GREY HAIR WITHOUT MAKING THAT SILLY SOUND... WHERE DID YOU SEE IT?

JUST THERE

EEEK!
70

WANT YOUR BACK DONE, LOVE?

I BEG YOUR PARDON!

ER. THE BACK OF THE HOUSE — WANT THE WINDOWS CLEANED?
138

IT'S MR FORBES — HE SAID I'M DUMB!
© EXPRESS NEWSPAPERS p.l.c. 1988

DAMN NERVE! GIVE ME THAT PHONE!

203
WHAT DO YOU MEAN, KATIE'S DUMB, FORBES? SHE CAN OUTSPEAK ANYONE!

WHAT WOULD WE DO IF WE HADN'T GOT...
... DALLAS, DYNASTY AND THE REST OF THE SOAPS?
51
I SUPPOSE WE'D WATCH TELEVISION
© EXPRESS NEWSPAPERS p.l.c. 1988

HERE'S A LIST OF DRESS SHOPS WE'LL CALL AT IN THAT ORDER, DARLING

IS IT NECESSARY TO CALL AT SHOPS IN A CERTAIN ORDER
218

OF COURSE IT IS — I LIKE TO PLAN MY IMPULSE BUYING

IT'S TIME ALL THE DIRT ON T.V. WAS CLEANED UP

YOU MEAN ALL THE DIRT WE SEE ON THE SCREEN?

NO, I MEAN ALL THE DUST WE SEE ON THE TOP
156

I'D LOVE A GLASS OF MILK, BUT I'M TOO LAZY TO GET IT

I CAN HEAR A KNOCKING SOUND DOWNSTAIRS
I'LL SEE WHAT IT IS
© EXPRESS NEWSPAPERS p.l.c. 1988

GET ME A GLASS OF MILK WHILE YOU'RE UP, DARLING

239
I DON'T KNOW WHAT THE KNOCKING WAS
I THINK IT WAS OPPORTUNITY, DARLING

WHAT HAVE YOU GOT TO SAY ABOUT THIS £127 PHONE BILL?
© EXPRESS NEWSPAPERS p.l.c. 1988

THERE'S A LOT I COULD SAY

BUT TALK IS CHEAP

WILFRED AND I WENT ON A SECOND HONEYMOON, BUT THE MAGIC WASN'T THERE

THAT'S SAD. SO IT WASN'T A THRILLING EXPERIENCE?
241

OH, IT WAS THRILLING WITH THE KNIFE-THROWER AND THE FIRE EATER, BUT THE PIER PAVILION DOESN'T HAVE A MAGICIAN ANYMORE
© EXPRESS NEWSPAPERS p.l.c. 1988

ANY PROBLEMS ON YOUR HOLIDAY? DID YOUR BAGGAGE TURN UP AT YOUR HOTEL?
YES, IT DID

YOU MUST HAVE BEEN PLEASED ABOUT THAT
WE WERE...
122

...IT WAS THE BAGGAGE THE AIRLINE LOST LAST YEAR
© EXPRESS NEWSPAPERS p.l.c. 1988

BARNEY'S USED CARS
THE PAINT'S CRACKING OFF IN PLACES, NEEDS TOUCHING UP, THE BODY'S NOT IN THE BEST OF SHAPE AND THE BUMPER STICKS OUT TOO FAR

WHICH CAR ARE YOU TALKING ABOUT?
© EXPRESS NEWSPAPERS p.l.c. 1988

246
I'M NOT SWEETHEART, I'M TALKING ABOUT MY MISSUS

DRY CLEANERS
LOVELY COAT THAT, DEARIE. WOULDN'T MIND ONE MYSELF
© EXPRESS NEWSPAPERS p.l.c. 1988

234
THANK YOU. YOU'VE CLEANED IT BEAUTIFULLY

JUST A MINUTE, LOVEY! DIDN'T LEAVE MY MONEY, KEYS AND CIGARETTES IN THE POCKETS, DID I?

WAILING ALIENS
THAT MOVIE WAS TOTALLY UNREALISTIC. YOU WOULD NEVER SEE CREATURES THAT LOOKED LIKE THAT
114
© EXPRESS NEWSPAPERS p.l.c. 1988
YOU WERE SAYING, DARLING
MADAM, YOU ARE THE MILLIONTH PERSON TO ENTER OUR STORE AND WE ARE GIVING YOU, ABSOLUTELY FREE, A CHURNWELL WASHING MACHINE!
© EXPRESS NEWSPAPERS p.l.c. 1988

TELL ME, MADAM, DO YOU COME INTO OUR STORE REGULARLY?
NO, ONLY WHEN I'M SHORT-CUTTING THROUGH IT ON MY WAY TO MONKS AND SPICERS STORE
91

BEEN WORKING HARD, DARLING?
I CERTAINLY HAVE, I'VE TURNED THE PLACE UPSIDE-DOWN TODAY

SPRING-CLEANING?

LOOKING FOR MY BOOK

© EXPRESS NEWSPAPERS p.l.c. 1988

HERE COMES THAT VAIN LITTLE VIXEN VICKI
FENDITTON NUDIST CAMP

237

MY ENGAGEMENT RING. I DON'T SUPPOSE EITHER OF YOU HAVE EVER SEEN ANYTHING SO EXPENSIVE AND RARE

RARE IS RIGHT, DEAR— YOU DON'T GET MANY OF THOSE IN A PACKET OF CORNFLAKES

© EXPRESS NEWSPAPERS p.l.c. 1988

IF THERE'S ONE THING I'VE LEARNT IN LIFE, IT IS THAT MONEY DOESN'T GROW ON TREES

YOU'RE DEAD RIGHT, DARLING

IT GROWS IN THE SHOPS YOU USE
202

I'M GIVING YOU A SMALL DINNER BECAUSE IT CONTAINS ANIMAL FAT AND THOSE LETHAL PRESERVATIVES, DYES AND EMULSIFIERS

AND I WANT TO KEEP YOU FIT SO THAT YOU'LL LIVE LONGER, BECAUSE I LOVE YOU SO VERY MUCH, MY DARLING

HOW MUCH OF THE MEAL DID YOU BURN, KATIE?
NEARLY ALL OF IT
199

WOULD YOUR LOVE DIE IF I LOST ALL MY MONEY, GLORIA?

OF COURSE NOT, DARLING

I'M SURE I COULD LOVE WHOEVER YOU LOST IT TO
100

SORRY, MISS — RULES AND REGULATIONS...
© EXPRESS NEWSPAPERS p.l.c. 1988

ONLY ONE-PIECE SWIMSUITS ARE ALLOWED ON THE BEACH

97
ALL RIGHT NOW?

HOW DID YOUR HOLIDAY GO?
STANDITTON NUDIST CLUB

127
KATIE THOUGHT THE SCENERY WAS DULL AND UNINTERESTING
WHAT WAS MISSING?
© EXPRESS NEWSPAPERS p.l.c. 1988

SHOPS

I HEAR A BURGLAR DOWNSTAIRS!
I'LL DEAL WITH HIM!
© EXPRESS NEWSPAPERS p.l.c. 1988

HAVE YOU TRIED ROBBING MONKS AND SPICERS WOMENS WEAR DEPARTMENT?
WHY SHOULD I DO THAT, SQUIRE?

BECAUSE THAT'S WHERE YOU'LL FIND OUR MONEY
128

IT WOULD BE NICE TO CELEBRATE MY BIRTHDAY TOMORROW. WHERE WILL YOU TAKE ME?
© EXPRESS NEWSPAPERS p.l.c. 1988

HOW ABOUT THAT NEW NIGHTCLUB?

205
HEY, I'VE JUST REALISED IT'S NOT YOUR BIRTHDAY TODAY!
I NEVER SAID IT WAS — I MERELY SAID IT WOULD BE NICE TO CELEBRATE IT

I'VE HAD LOTS OF COMPLIMENTS ABOUT MY DRESS, BUT THEN, WITH MY TASTE IT'S TO BE EXPECTED

MIND YOU, IT'S JUST SOMETHING I THREW ON
© EXPRESS NEWSPAPERS p.l.c. 1988

206
WHAT A PITY HER AIM IS SO GOOD

WILL YOU COME OUT OF THAT DARNED BATHROOM! I HAVE TO GET TO THE OFFICE!

SHE'LL BE AGES— I'D BETTER GET MY BREAKFAST!
© EXPRESS NEWSPAPERS p.l.c. 1988

SHE HASN'T PUT A SHIRT OUT FOR ME!

229
HERE'S YOUR BRIEFCASE —WHERE WOULD MEN BE WITHOUT US WOMEN BEHIND THEM?

MY WIFE GAVE ME AN ULTIMATUM. GIVE UP GOLF, SHE SAID, OR I'LL PACK AND LEAVE YOU AND NEVER COME BACK

AND I'M BEGINNING TO THINK SHE MEANS IT
WHY'S THAT?
© EXPRESS NEWSPAPERS p.l.c. 1988

SHE'S BEEN GONE TWENTY-TWO YEARS
230

ROSY
LOOK AT THAT! IT'S BLATANT EXPLOITATION OF WOMEN!

I PAY THE STRIPPERS £2,000 A WEEK
© EXPRESS NEWSPAPERS p.l.c. 1988

THEY TAKE £2,000 A WEEK? THAT'S BLATANT EXPLOITATION OF MEN!
215

I RECOMMEND THE STRAWBERRY SURPRISE, SIR
ALL RIGHT, I'LL TRY IT
© EXPRESS NEWSPAPERS p.l.c. 1988

BUT THIS IS JUST STRAWBERRIES! WHERE'S THE SURPRISE?

I'LL BRING THE BILL FOR THEM, SIR
216

I WAS SIXTEEN STONE WHEN THE OLD SKINFLINT MARRIED ME ...
© EXPRESS NEWSPAPERS p.l.c. 1988

... THEN I GOT DOWN TO EIGHT STONE

SO HE WENT TO THE REGISTRY OFFICE AND DEMANDED HALF THE LICENCE FEE BACK
192

THAT PHONE CALL'S COST US A PACKET. YOU'VE BEEN ON FOR AN HOUR. WHO DID YOU CALL?

DEBBIE. TO GIVE HER ALL THE LATEST NEWS AND GOSSIP ...
© EXPRESS NEWSPAPERS p.l.c. 1988

... AND TO TELL HER I'LL SEE HER IN TEN MINUTES
191

THAT DARNED POSTMAN KNOCKS EVERY MORNING KNOWING I'LL BE IN THIS NEGLIGEE — EVERY MORNING EXCEPT SATURDAY
© EXPRESS NEWSPAPERS p.l.c. 1988

THERE'S A LETTER IN THE DAILY STAR FROM L.H. WHITAKER OF LEEDS, WHO COMPLAINS THAT YOU SPOIL THINGS EVERY SATURDAY BY PUTTING YOUR CLOTHES ON

GOOD HEAVENS, DO YOU SUPPOSE L.H. WHITAKER IS OUR POSTMAN?
227

THAT CAT TINA HAS MESMERISED MY HUSBAND! SHE'S TWISTING HIM ROUND HER LITTLE FINGER!
© EXPRESS NEWSPAPERS p.l.c. 1988

AND ALL THE TIME SHE'S GLOATING AT ME, KNOWING SHE'S GOT HIM, THE SADISTIC LITTLE SO-AND-SO!
BUT YOU MUST DO SOMETHING ABOUT HER!

HOW CAN I — SHE'S MY BEST FRIEND
228

YOU'VE GOT A CHOICE, DARLING— YOU CAN WATCH THAT FOOTBALL MATCH OR SPEND TEN MINUTES WITH ME
© EXPRESS NEWSPAPERS p.l.c. 1988

YOU'RE WONDERFUL, DARLIN'! WHAT MADE YOU SPARE ME TEN MINUTES?
89

HALF-TIME

I'LL NEVER UNDERSTAND MEN AS LONG AS I LIVE
WHY'S THAT?
© EXPRESS NEWSPAPERS p.l.c. 1988

BECAUSE YOU'RE ALL DITHERING INDECISIVE CREATURES. BY THE TIME YOU'VE MADE UP YOUR MIND ABOUT SOMETHING ...

... A WOMAN'S MADE HERS UP AND CHANGED IT A DOZEN TIMES
134

MY DRIVING INSTRUCTOR SAID TODAY THAT THERE WAS A FAULT WITH THE CAR THAT NEEDED TO BE ELIMINATED
© EXPRESS NEWSPAPERS p.l.c. 1988

WHAT FORM DID THIS FAULT TAKE?
136

HE SAID IT TOOK A 38-24-36 FORM

LIKE MY NEW BIKINI, DARLING?

IT COST £97
© EXPRESS NEWSPAPERS p.l.c. 1988

137
£97? THAT MUST BE £5 FOR THE BIKINI AND £92 FOR THE BOX!

I'M ALWAYS LATE FOR WORK, BECAUSE THE DARNED BUS GOES STRAIGHT PAST, SO I DECIDED TO STOP IT YESTERDAY
© EXPRESS NEWSPAPERS p.l.c. 1988

I SLIPPED MY TOP OFF AND RAISED MY SKIRT A MILE OR TWO
DID IT STOP?

IT DID WHEN IT HIT THE BRICK WALL
149

WHICH DO YOU THINK IS THE MOST POPULAR SPECTATOR SPORT?
© EXPRESS NEWSPAPERS p.l.c. 1988

I'M NOT SURE, DARLING ...

...BUT I THINK IT'S WINDOW CLEANING
85

IRONIC, ISN'T IT?

WHAT IS?
151

THIS HOLIDAY WAS PAID FOR WITH THE MONEY WE SAVED FOR A RAINY DAY

YOU'VE BOUGHT AN EXPENSIVE EXERCISE BIKE! YOU KNOW WE CAN'T AFFORD IT!
BUT I THOUGHT YOU WANTED ME TO BUY IT, DARLING

WHAT MADE YOU THINK THAT?
WELL, WHEN I SUGGESTED I BUY IT, YOU SAID ....

ON YOUR BIKE!
74

DARLING, WOULDN'T YOU LIKE A HOLIDAY...
...WHERE YOU CAN RELAX FOR TWO WEEKS IN PEACE AND QUIET, WHERE THE SILENCE IS UNBROKEN?
© EXPRESS NEWSPAPERS p.l.c. 1988

236
NO, I'D RATHER HAVE A HOLIDAY WITH YOU

I BELIEVE IN REINCARNATION. I THINK WE COME BACK IN ANOTHER FORM

WHAT FORM WOULD YOU LIKE TO RETURN IN?
© EXPRESS NEWSPAPERS p.l.c. 1988

BO DEREK'S
163

THAT GLAMOROUS FILM STAR IN THE SOAP OPERA — SHE'S LOST HALF A STONE

HOW DID SHE MANAGE THAT?
146

SHE TOOK HER MAKE-UP OFF

THE JORDANS DECIDED TO MOVE TO A MUCH MORE EXPENSIVE HOUSE
DID THEY FIND WHAT THEY WANTED?

YES, AFTER THREE MONTHS, WITH PRICES RISING THE WAY THEY ARE, THEIR HOUSE WAS SO EXPENSIVE ...
160

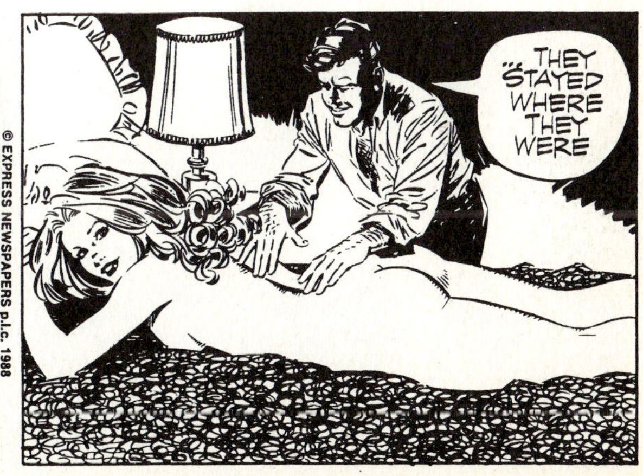

...THEY STAYED WHERE THEY WERE

170

A STAR READER HAS WRITTEN ASKING WHY YOU'VE NEVER GOT ANY CLOTHES ON

I SHOULD HAVE THOUGHT IT WAS OBVIOUS. TELL THE READERS WHY YOU'RE ALWAYS NUDE, KATIE

BECAUSE I HAVEN'T GOT A THING TO WEAR!

© EXPRESS NEWSPAPERS p.l.c. 1988

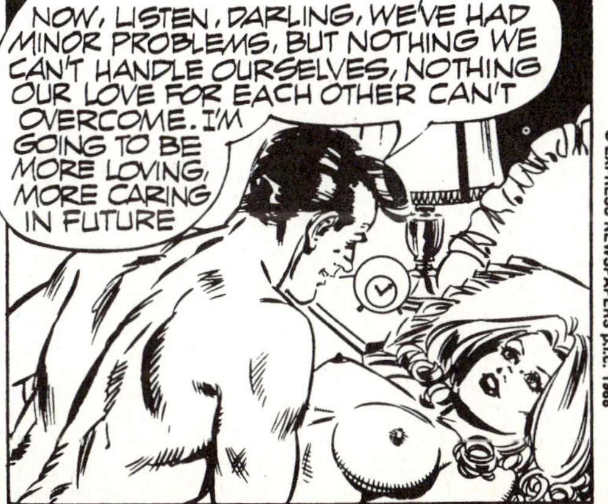

The top row of panels:

WOULD YOU MOVE YOUR HEAD TO THE LEFT, KATIE?
NEIGHBOURS

AM I OBSTRUCTING YOUR VIEW, DARLING?
© EXPRESS NEWSPAPERS p.l.c. 1988

NO, BUT IF YOU MOVE YOUR HEAD TO THE LEFT, YOU WILL BE
167

I HEARD A BURGLAR IN THE NIGHT AND WENT DOWNSTAIRS IN MY SEE-THROUGH NIGHTIE
© EXPRESS NEWSPAPERS p.l.c. 1988

HOW FRIGHTENING!

176
IT MUST HAVE BEEN — HE TOOK ONE LOOK, SCREAMED AND BOLTED

YOU WERE TALKING IN YOUR SLEEP AGAIN
WHY DIDN'T YOU STOP ME?

I COULDN'T GET A WORD IN EDGEWAYS

TERRIBLE SCENES THEY'VE BEEN SHOWING ON T.V. THESE PAST FEW MONTHS! THEY MUST HAVE ALL KINDS OF ADVERSE EFFECTS ON YOUNG MINDS

YOU'RE TALKING ABOUT SEX AND VIOLENCE?

I'M TALKING ABOUT ENGLISH CRICKET

DO YOU LOVE ME, BEN?
OF COURSE I DO, DARLING. YOU CAN HAVE THE MOON AND THE STARS

YOU'RE SO WONDERFUL AND I LOVE YOU SO MUCH, BUT I DON'T EXPECT THE IMPOSSIBLE ...

... I'LL SETTLE FOR A FUR COAT AND A NEW DRESS
223

I DON'T WANT TO HEAR YOUR EXCUSE FOR COMING HOME AT THIS HOUR IN THAT STATE!

OH, COME ON KATIE, BE FAIR!

I'VE BEEN WORKING ON IT FOR THE PAST HOUR!
224

GREAT AUNT EDNA CALLED ME EVERYTHING FOR NOT SENDING HER A CHRISTMAS PRESENT LAST YEAR AND SAID IT'S NOT TOO LATE TO MAKE AMENDS

SO I'M SENDING HER A PRESENT
WHAT ARE YOU SENDING?

LAST YEAR'S CALENDAR
1987
© EXPRESS NEWSPAPERS p.l.c. 1988
189

OH, YES, MADAM, IT IS YOU!
© EXPRESS NEWSPAPERS p.l.c. 1988

£117!

AND THE PRICE IS ME!
190

I THINK I'LL TRY ORDINARY SOAP POWDER TOMORROW
WHY?

WELL, IT'S BEEN ADVERTISED ON T.V. FOR A LONG TIME...
139

... AND IT'S OUTLASTED SEVERAL OF ITS COMPETITORS, SO IT MUST BE GOOD
© EXPRESS NEWSPAPERS p.l.c. 1988

WHAT'S GOING ON?
© EXPRESS NEWSPAPERS p.l.c. 1988

I'M REPLACING MY OLD WARDROBE WITH A NEW ONE, DARLING

OH, FOR A MOMENT I THOUGHT YOU WERE GOING OFF ON HOLIDAY
180

© EXPRESS NEWSPAPERS p.l.c. 1988

© EXPRESS NEWSPAPERS p.l.c. 1988

GIVE ME A HAND TO MAKE THE BED, BEN, AND THEN I'LL HELP YOU
OKAY

THERE WE ARE — ALL DONE

THANK YOU, DARLING. NOW I'LL HELP YOU TO DO THE WASHING-UP AND THE IRONING
111

WE'RE IN FOR A DREARY EVENING AT THE PUGHSONS. THEY'LL BE FULL OF BORING TALK ABOUT THEIR HOLIDAY

YES, AND THERE WILL BE BORING PHOTOS AND EVEN MORE BORING FILMS TO SUFFER

RUTH, WE WON'T BE ABLE TO COME TONIGHT— WE'RE SUFFERING FROM POST-HOLIDAY DEPRESSION
112

© EXPRESS NEWSPAPERS p.l.c. 1988

DO I COOK LIKE YOUR MOTHER USED TO, DARLING?
OF COURSE YOU DO, SWEETHEART

WHAT A LOVELY THING TO SAY! BUT HOW CAN YOU BE SURE?
© EXPRESS NEWSPAPERS p.l.c. 1988

BECAUSE I GET INDIGESTION LIKE MY FATHER USED TO
83

I SEE FILM STAR FIFI LAMORE'S JUST ARRIVED IN THIS COUNTRY
SHE MUST BE BETWEEN MOVIES

NO, SHE'S OVER HERE TO MAKE A MOVIE
84

THEN SHE MUST BE BETWEEN FACE-LIFTS
© EXPRESS NEWSPAPERS p.l.c. 1988

WHY DON'T WE HAVE A SECOND HONEYMOON, DARLING?

GOOD IDEA. WE'LL START JUST AS SOON AS ...

...WE'VE FINISHED THE FIRST ONE
123

ACCORDING TO THIS REPORT, BY THE AGE OF 18, MOST AMERICAN CHILDREN HAVE SPENT TWO YEARS WATCHING TELEVISION

AND PROBABLY SPENT THE OTHER 16 YEARS ...

...WONDERING WHY THEY BOTHERED
124

YES, I'LL TAKE IT
SHALL I TAKE THE PRICE TAG OFF, MADAM?

NOT YET. THE TIME TO TAKE THE PRICE TAG OFF IS ...

... AFTER YOUR FRIENDS HAVE SEEN IT AND BEFORE YOUR HUSBAND HAS SEEN IT
162

PAUL SURPRISED ME ON MY BIRTHDAY
WHAT DID HE BUY YOU?

A COUPLE OF HANKIES
YOU CALL THAT A SURPRISE?

119
YOU DO WHEN YOU'RE EXPECTING A NEW COAT

WHAT BECAME OF THAT AMBITIOUS FRIEND OF YOURS— THE ONE WHO WANTED TO BECOME A WORLD-FAMOUS ACTRESS?

FIONA? SHE TRIED BUT FOUND SHE HAD NO ACTING TALENT WHATSOEVER
THAT'S SAD. WHAT'S SHE DOING NOW?
© EXPRESS NEWSPAPERS p.l.c. 1988
63

SHE'S GOT A BIG PART IN A SOAP OPERA

I DON'T KNOW WHY SILLY VAIN WOMEN HAVE TO HIDE THEIR AGE. I DON'T CARE WHO KNOWS I'M 35
© EXPRESS NEWSPAPERS p.l.c. 1988

SHE'S VERY BRAVE TO ADMIT SHE'S 35

129
YES, BUT SHE SHOULD BE TEN YEARS BRAVER

I ALMOST BUMPED INTO THAT NATTERBOX MRS GROOME IN THE BANK TODAY. THERE'S NO ESCAPE ONCE SHE STARTS TALKING

YOU SHOULD HAVE MADE A HASTY WITHDRAWAL

I THOUGHT YOU'D SAY THAT, DARLING, SO I DID — THIS IS WHAT I BOUGHT WITH IT
200

I MANAGED TO GET A LIFT HOME, DARLING

A LIFT? BUT YOU HAD THE CAR! HOW COULD YOU POSSIBLY WANT...

...A LIFT?

DO YOU WANT AN ESTIMATE, SQUIRE, OR JUST THE BILL WHEN WE'RE FINISHED?

WHAT'S THE DIFFERENCE?
© EXPRESS NEWSPAPERS p.l.c. 1988

166
ABOUT £57

I'M GOING TO SURPRISE YOU WITH A BUNCH OF FLOWERS TONIGHT, DARLING
© EXPRESS NEWSPAPERS p.l.c. 1988

BUT NOW YOU'VE TOLD ME, IT WON'T BE A SURPRISE, WILL IT?
NO, I SUPPOSE NOT
178

TELL YOU WHAT — SURPRISE ME WITH DIAMOND EARRINGS INSTEAD

DON'T YOU EVER DO ANY HOUSEWORK?
ARISTIDES HAD NO TROUBLE GETTING A JOB IN THIS COUNTRY
ARISTIDES? BUT HE SPEAKS HARDLY A WORD OF ENGLISH AND THE LITTLE HE DOES SPEAK IS GARBLED AND INCOMPREHENSIBLE. WHAT JOB DID HE GET?
© EXPRESS NEWSPAPERS p.l.c. 1985

THE TOP OF THIS TELEVISION'S THICK WITH DUST
TRAIN ANNOUNCER FOR BRITISH RAIL
© EXPRESS NEWSPAPERS p.l.c. 1985

DON'T TOUCH IT— I'VE WRITTEN A NOTE IN THE DUST TO REMIND ME THAT I START ATTENDING HOUSE-CLEANING CLASSES NEXT WEEK
93
94

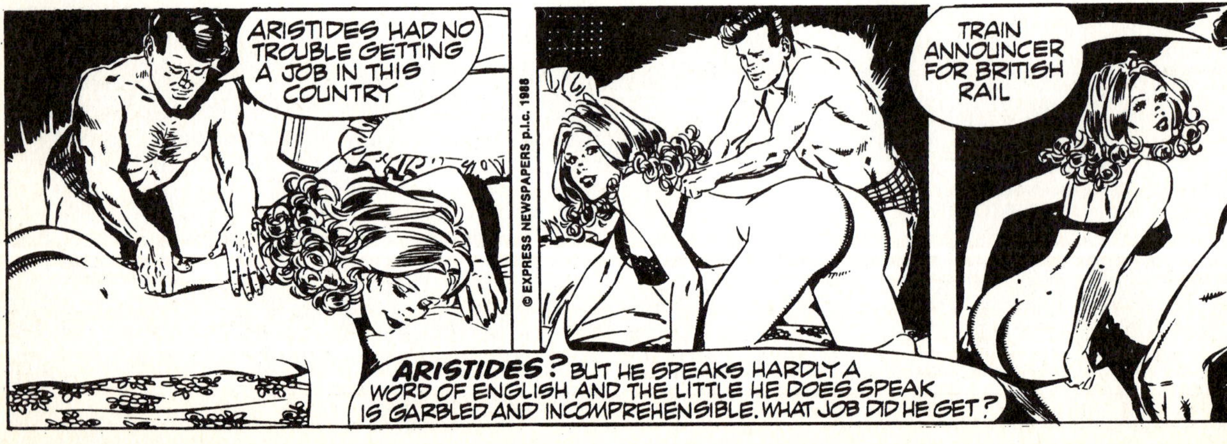

THAT ITALIAN BOY I TOLD YOU ABOUT— HE WAS TWENTY MINUTES LATE FOR OUR DATE

TWENTY MINUTES? I BET YOU WERE FURIOUS?

I WAS ABSOLUTELY MAD! I GAVE HIM HELL WHEN I ARRIVED TEN MINUTES LATER!
115

I WANT YOU TO TURN LEFT AT THE NEXT JUNCTION
DO YOU LIKE MY PERFUME AND MY HAIRDO?
© EXPRESS NEWSPAPERS p.l.c. 1988

STOP JUST HERE AND DO A THREE-POINT TURN
WHAT DO YOU THINK OF MY DRESS— ISN'T IT LOVELY?

116
HOW DID YOUR DRIVING TEST GO?
I DID AS YOU SUGGESTED AND TRIED HARD TO IMPRESS THE EXAMINER, BUT I STILL FAILED!

I HAD A RESTLESS NIGHT LAST NIGHT— HARDLY A WINK OF SLEEP

YOU'RE LUCKY, KATIE . . .
© EXPRESS NEWSPAPERS p.l.c. 1988

. . . WITH A HUSBAND LIKE MINE, I GET NOTHING BUT REST ALL NIGHT
101

WHY DON'T WE HAVE A SELF-CATERING HOLIDAY, DARLING ?

MAKE UP YOUR MIND. . . .
© EXPRESS NEWSPAPERS p.l.c. 1988

. . . DO WE HAVE SELF-CATERING OR DO WE HAVE A HOLIDAY ?
102

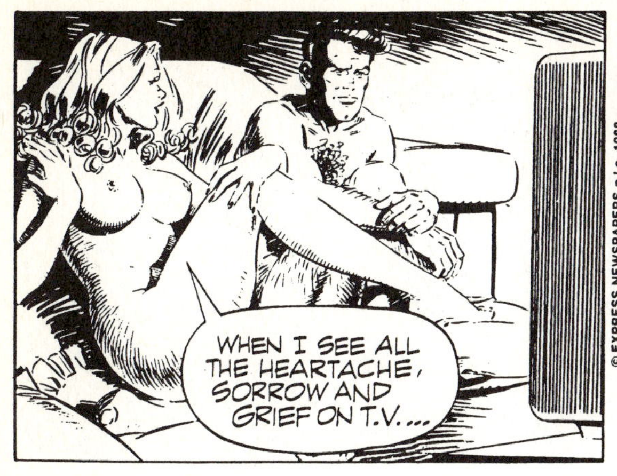

WHEN I SEE ALL THE HEARTACHE, SORROW AND GRIEF ON T.V. ....

... I FEEL SICK

YEAH, DYNASTY AFFECTS ME THAT WAY TOO
71

THIS IS BERNARD HOLDSWORTH'S LATEST NOVEL — HE MUST BE THE MOST PROLIFIC OF BRITISH WRITERS

MY WIFE'S A MORE PROLIFIC WRITER THAN HE IS — SHE'S INTO HER 700th BOOK
REALLY? WHAT DOES SHE WRITE?

72
CHEQUES

THOSE FANS SHE'S GOT ARE TOO BIG. I'D LIKE TO SEE HER USING SMALLER ONES
© EXPRESS NEWSPAPERS p.l.c. 1988

GEORGE! WHAT MAKES YOU SAY SUCH A TERRIBLE THING?
80

THE DRAUGHT I'M GETTING DOWN THE BACK OF MY NECK!

WE'RE OFF ABROAD FOR A BREAK TOMORROW. WE GO FROM HEATHROW AND I'M SCARED STIFF!
© EXPRESS NEWSPAPERS p.l.c. 1988

KATIE, THERE'S NOTHING TO IT. YOU SHOULDN'T BE SCARED OF FLYING
88

FLYING? WHO'S SCARED OF FLYING! I'M TALKING ABOUT EATING HEATHROW FOOD
EGON RONAY SLAMS HEATHROW FOOD

NOT ANOTHER NEW DRESS!
OF COURSE NOT — I'VE HAD IT FOR AGES

I CAN SEE THE LABEL — YOU GOT IT FROM MISS SINDY'S AND THAT SHOP'S ONLY BEEN OPEN TWO MONTHS

231
DARLING, WHEN A WOMAN HASN'T HAD A NEW DRESS FOR TWO MONTHS, THAT'S AGES

BEN, WHAT IS INFLATION?

IT'S A RISE IN PRICES RESULTING FROM AN INCREASE IN THE RATIO OF CURRENCY TO THE GOODS AVAILABLE

WELL, COULD YOU PUT A RISE IN PRICES IN MY FRONT TYRE FOR ME — IT'S A BIT FLAT
77

ON A MOTORWAY, A LORRY BURST INTO FLAMES, COOKING ITS 38-TON LOAD OF STEAK AND KIDNEY
I WONDER IF THE DRIVER DID IT DELIBERATELY...

...TO AVOID EATING AT A SERVICE STATION
118

DID I TELL YOU ANDY WALKED OUT ON ME — JUST UP AND LEFT?

DIDN'T STEVE AND MIKE LEAVE YOU TOO? YOU DON'T SEEM TO HAVE MUCH LUCK WITH MEN

LISTEN, I'M SO UNLUCKY THAT IF A MAN CAME IN THROUGH MY BEDROOM WINDOW, IT WOULD ONLY BE TO LEAVE A BOX OF MILK TRAY
108

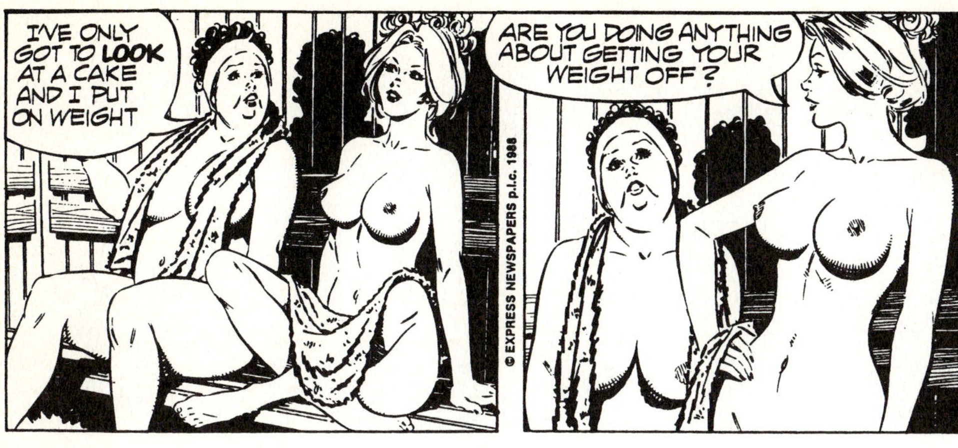

I'VE ONLY GOT TO LOOK AT A CAKE AND I PUT ON WEIGHT
ARE YOU DOING ANYTHING ABOUT GETTING YOUR WEIGHT OFF?
© EXPRESS NEWSPAPERS p.l.c. 1986

WELL, I TRIED LOOKING AT AN EXERCISE BIKE, BUT NOTHING HAPPENED
104

MY DRIVING INSTRUCTOR TOLD ME I OUGHT TO USE THE REAR VIEW MIRROR MORE

SO I TOLD HIM IT WASN'T NECESSARY...
© EXPRESS NEWSPAPERS p.l.c. 1986

...AS I WAS WELL AWARE OF THE TURMOIL I LEAVE BEHIND
99

THIS IS MY HUSBAND HERBERT
HELLO, HERBERT

I GOT HIM AT A MARRIAGE BUREAU, YOU KNOW

56
IT MUST HAVE BEEN IN THE SALES
© EXPRESS NEWSPAPERS p.l.c. 1988

DOES YOUR HUSBAND STILL LAUGH AT YOUR EFFORTS WHEN YOU WRITE ROMANTIC STORIES?
MAVERHAM BADMINTON CLUB
© EXPRESS NEWSPAPERS p.l.c. 1988

NO, I PUT A STOP TO HIS LAUGHTER
HOW?

53
I WRITE COMEDY NOW

I WROTE TO THE POST OFFICE A FORTNIGHT AGO, COMPLAINING ABOUT THE POOR DELIVERY SERVICE

NOTHING HAPPENED SO I PHONED THEM YESTERDAY
WHAT DID THEY SAY?

THEY DENIED A POOR SERVICE AND SAID THEY'D DEAL WITH MY LETTER WHEN THEY RECEIVED IT
121

SO PARLIAMENT'S GOING TO BE TELEVISED

LIVE?

HALF-ALIVE
57

HARRY'S SON TURNED OUT TO BE NO GOOD. HE'S DECEITFUL AND DISHONEST, GREEDY AND LUSTFUL
© EXPRESS NEWSPAPERS p.l.c. 1988

HE OUGHT TO TURN TO RELIGION

HE DID— NOW HE'S DOING NICELY AS AN EVANGELIST
65

THIS BILL FOR CAR REPAIRS—IT'S NOT REALLY £413, IS IT?
© EXPRESS NEWSPAPERS p.l.c. 1988

OF COURSE NOT, SILLY
YOU HAD ME WORRIED FOR A MOMENT

KNOWING YOU'RE SUPERSTITIOUS, I TOLD THEM TO MAKE IT £414
68

YOU MEAN INTENSIVE CARE
MY OLD MAN GOT IN A PUNCH-UP IN THE PUB. TOOK A RIGHT PASTING. NOW HE'S IN EXPENSIVE CARE
© EXPRESS NEWSPAPERS p.l.c. 1988

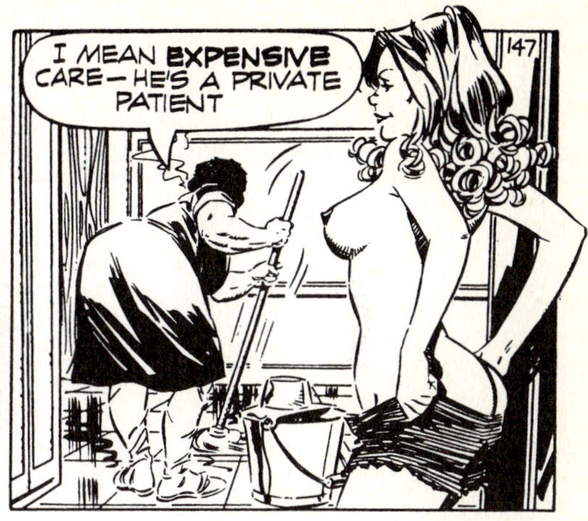
I MEAN EXPENSIVE CARE — HE'S A PRIVATE PATIENT
147

HI, DARLING. I'M HOME
© EXPRESS NEWSPAPERS p.l.c. 1988

GOOD GRIEF! HAVEN'T YOU GOT UP YET? IT'S SIX O'CLOCK IN THE EVENING! WHAT ABOUT DINNER?

I'LL DO IT PRESENTLY — AFTER I'VE HAD A LIE-IN
61

DAVID STILL DOESN'T SEEM TO NOTICE ME. I'VE DONE ALL I CAN TO PUT ACROSS THAT I'M A WONDERFUL PERSON

WHAT DO YOU DO TO GET A MAN TO NOTICE YOU?

220
TELL HIM WHAT A WONDERFUL PERSON HE IS
© EXPRESS NEWSPAPERS p.l.c. 1988

ANDREW AND I CAN'T HAVE CHILDREN, YOU KNOW
OH, NO! THAT'S TERRIBLE! DID THE DOCTOR TELL YOU?
NO, THE MAN AT THE BUILDING SOCIETY, WHO GAVE US THE HEFTY MORTGAGE TOLD US
© EXPRESS NEWSPAPERS p.l.c. 1988
73

SO MORE WAGES PUTS UP COSTS, WHICH LEADS TO MORE WAGE DEMANDS AND SO PRICES CONTINUE TO RISE
WELL, I'VE BEEN A CLEVER LITTLE GIRL. I WENT OUT AND BOUGHT LOTS OF CLOTHES ...
THAT'S AN INFLATIONARY SPIRAL
247

... AS A HEDGE AGAINST INFLATION
© EXPRESS NEWSPAPERS p.l.c. 1988

IS THAT YOU, KATIE?
© EXPRESS NEWSPAPERS p.l.c. 1988

I THINK I KNOW WHAT WE CAN SPEND MY TAX REBATE ON
150

WHAT TAX REBATE, DARLING?

THIS IS PRETTY STEAMY STUFF
I READ THE BOOK OF THIS MOVIE AND THIS SCENE WAS COMPLETELY DIFFERENT
© EXPRESS NEWSPAPERS p.l.c. 1988

WHAT HAPPENED IN THE BOOK?

SHE HAD A HEADACHE
64

THEY TALK ABOUT ELIMINATING T.V. VIOLENCE, YET THEY'RE GOING TO CLOSE A PROGRAMME...
© EXPRESS NEWSPAPERS p.l.c. 1988
STAR SPORT

...THAT'S FULL OF HUMOUR AND GOOD ACTING AND TOTALLY DEVOID OF VIOLENCE
WHAT'S IT CALLED?

WRESTLING
THE STAR
152

I'VE BEEN FOLLOWING THE OIL CRISIS ON T.V. NOTHING COULD BE MORE DEPRESSING
© EXPRESS NEWSPAPERS p.l.c. 1988

THEN YOU SHOULDN'T WATCH THE NEWS

I WASN'T — I WAS WATCHING DALLAS
69

KATIE DROVE TO THE SUPERMARKET FOR SIX SMALL ITEMS AND THE COST WAS £87
© EXPRESS NEWSPAPERS p.l.c. 1988

£87? YOU WERE ROBBED!

NOT REALLY — I THOUGHT THE BILL FOR THE CAR REPAIRS WAS QUITE REASONABLE
133

© EXPRESS NEWSPAPERS p.l.c. 1988

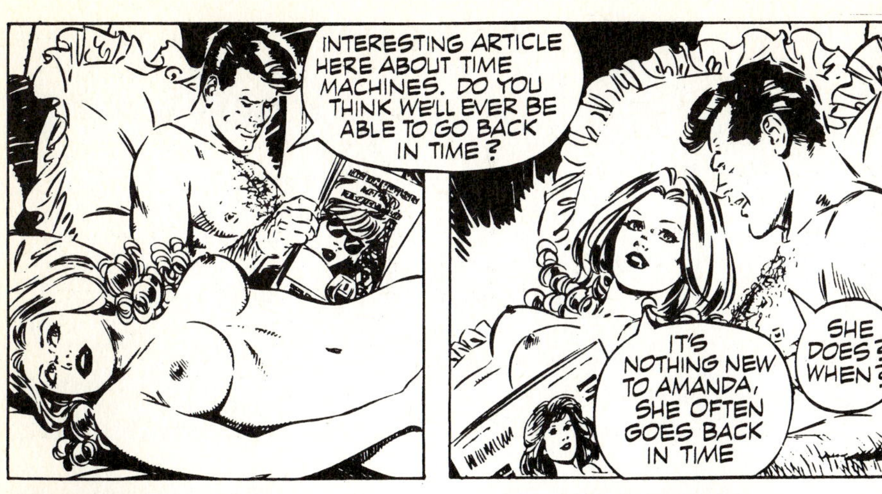

INTERESTING ARTICLE HERE ABOUT TIME MACHINES. DO YOU THINK WE'LL EVER BE ABLE TO GO BACK IN TIME?
IT'S NOTHING NEW TO AMANDA, SHE OFTEN GOES BACK IN TIME
SHE DOES? WHEN?

ON HER BIRTHDAY

148

IT'S LEFTOVERS, DARLING
BUT I HAD LEFTOVERS YESTERDAY!

YES, BUT YOU DIDN'T EAT IT ALL, SO THESE ARE THE LEFTOVERS LEFT OVER FROM THE LEFTOVERS

LEFT OVER LEFTOVERS? I'D BETTER EAT IT ALL OR TOMORROW IT'S **LEFT OVER** LEFT OVER LEFTOVERS!

155

APPARENTLY, SWIMMING IMPROVES YOUR LOVE LIFE, DARLING. DO YOU THINK WE OUGHT TO TAKE UP SWIMMING?
THE STAR
SWIM FOR YOUR LOVE LIVES

WE COULD DO ...
© EXPRESS NEWSPAPERS p.l.c. 1988

... BUT THINK OF ALL THE TIME WE'D BE WASTING
109

I TRAVELLED SOUTH LAST WEEK AND THE TRAFFIC WAS TERRIBLE! I'VE NEVER KNOWN SUCH CONGESTION!

BUMPER TO BUMPER, EH?
96

NO, PLANE NOSE TO PLANE TAIL — I'M TALKING ABOUT THE AIR LANES OVER HEATHROW
© EXPRESS NEWSPAPERS p.l.c. 1988

APPARENTLY 70% OF THE WORLD'S POPULATION HAVE NO NEWSPAPERS, T.V. OR RADIO

SO WHAT DO THEY DO FOR AMUSEMENT?

I DON'T KNOW, BUT IT'S PROBABLY INCREASED FROM 70% TO 80% BY NOW
© EXPRESS NEWSPAPERS p.l.c. 1988
143

144
I SEE ANITA HAS LATCHED ON TO BEN

JUST LOOK AT HER ENORMOUS EARRINGS
© EXPRESS NEWSPAPERS p.l.c. 1988

YES, SHE'D DO ANYTHING TO ATTRACT ATTENTION

MR. KIMBERLEY'S WIFE JUST HAD SIX BABIES!
SIX! I MUST TELL HIM
MATERNITY

ROGER, YOU'LL SOON BE HEARING THE PATTER OF FEET
© EXPRESS NEWSPAPERS p.l.c. 1988

IT WILL BE THE T.V. AND PRESS PEOPLE COMING TO INTERVIEW YOU
117

THERE'S A REPEAT OF THAT SOAP OPERA YOU SLEPT THROUGHT LAST TIME IT WAS ON
© EXPRESS NEWSPAPERS p.l.c. 1988

YOU MISSED ALL THE EXCITEMENT AND DRAMA, THE TENSION AND HEARTACHE. WANT TO SEE IT NOW?
GOOD IDEA. IT SOUNDS GREAT!
219

NNNN

DID YOU SEE YOUR BOSS ABOUT THE RISE, DARLING?
YES, I TOLD HIM I WANTED MORE MONEY AS I WAS DOING THE WORK OF TWO MEN
WHAT DID HE SAY?
HE WANTED TO KNOW WHO THE TWO MEN WERE SO THAT HE COULD SACK THEM AS THEY WEREN'T DOING ENOUGH WORK
110
© EXPRESS NEWSPAPERS p.l.c. 1988

THAT TAKES CARE OF MY EYES
NOW FOR THE REST OF MY MAKE-UP
AND THAT SHOULD TAKE CARE OF THE FIRST WEEK OF THE HOLIDAY
© EXPRESS NEWSPAPERS p.l.c. 1988
HOLIDAY TRAVEL
106

IN OUR NEXT PROGRAMME, WE TAKE A LOOK AT THE UNDERTAKING PROFESSION
© EXPRESS NEWSPAPERS p.l.c. 1988

LET'S TURN IT OFF. IT SOUNDS A BIT MORBID
105

YES, FOR A MOMENT I THOUGHT HE WAS GOING TO SAY 'THIS PROGRAMME WAS FILMED BEFORE A DEAD STUDIO AUDIENCE'

THIS PHONE BILL'S HIGH AGAIN
© EXPRESS NEWSPAPERS p.l.c. 1988

DID YOU DO AS I ASKED AND CUT DOWN ON PHONE CALLS?

YES, I DID, DARLING—I ASKED ALL MY FRIENDS NOT TO RING ME SO OFTEN
130

WITH ALL THE SADNESS AND SUFFERING THERE IS IN LIFE, DON'T YOU THINK EVERYONE SHOULD LIVE FOR TODAY?

OF COURSE, DARLING. AND THAT'S WHAT YOU AND I MUST DO — LIVE FOR TODAY
245
© EXPRESS NEWSPAPERS p.l.c. 1988

WELL, NOW THAT YOU AGREE, LET ME SHOW YOU WHAT I BOUGHT TODAY

HAVING ANY SUCCESS WITH RICHARD?
YES, I CONSTANTLY HINTED ABOUT MARRIAGE AND NOW I SHALL BE WALKING UP THE AISLE ON SATURDAY

THAT'S WONDERFUL! YOU'LL MAKE A LOVELY BRIDE
© EXPRESS NEWSPAPERS p.l.c. 1988
243

NO, I'LL MAKE A LOVELY BRIDESMAID — HE'S MARRYING JULIA

THE NEXT PROGRAMME, ABOUT EINSTEIN'S THEORY OF RELATIVITY, HAS BEEN SHOWN BEFORE...

SO IF YOU FAILED TO UNDERSTAND THE GENIUS'S THEORY THEN, HERE IS AN OPPORTUNITY...
95

...TO FAIL TO UNDERSTAND IT AGAIN
© EXPRESS NEWSPAPERS p.l.c. 1988

LIZ! WE HAVEN'T HAD A LONG TELEPHONE CHAT FOR TWO DAYS...WE WERE GOING TO BUY A PORSCHE, A WEEKEND COTTAGE AND A FLAT IN LONDON

YOU'RE NOT GOING TO NOW?
© EXPRESS NEWSPAPERS p.l.c. 1988

NO, BEN'S GOING TO PAY THE TELEPHONE BILL INSTEAD
201

I WAS ABSOLUTELY LIVID! OUR FLIGHT WAS DELAYED EIGHT HOURS! I THOUGHT WE'D NEVER TAKE OFF!
© EXPRESS NEWSPAPERS p.l.c. 1988

HELLO, KATIE. DID YOUR HOLIDAY GET OFF TO A FLYING START?

181
SHOWERS
I WONDER WHY SHE SCREAMED WHEN I ASKED THAT

DO I LOOK ALLURING, PROVOCATIVE AND TOTALLY IRRESISTIBLE?

YOU CERTAINLY DO, DARLING
© EXPRESS NEWSPAPERS p.l.c. 1988

WHAT WAS FOR DINNER?
183

THAT YOUNG ASSISTANT OF YOURS WAS WATCHING ME TAKE A BATH!

NO SWEAT, LOVE. VERY MORAL, KEVIN IS. WHEN HE WAS LOOKING AT YOU, HE WAS DRESSING YOU WITH HIS EYES
182

ISN'T IT LOVELY, DARLING? QUITE CHEAP TOO

I BOUGHT IT OUT OF THE HOUSEKEEPING
SO WHAT DID IT COST?

ONLY YOUR DINNERS FOR A FEW WEEKS
184